ARCTIC APPETIZERS

Studying Food Webs in the Arctic

GWENDOLYN HOOKS

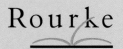

Rourke

Publishing LLC

Vero Beach, Florida 32964

www.rourkepublishing.com

Project Assistance:
The author thanks Carin Ashjian, Ph.D. Woods Hole Oceanographic Institution, Massachusetts, Julie Lundgren, and the team at Blue Door Publishing.

Photo credits: Page 4 © Condor 36; Page 5 © noaa; Page 6 © Galyna Andrushko, National Oceanic and Atmospheric Administration, Uwe Kils; Page 7 © Dirk-Jan Mattaar, Condor 36, Matt Ragen, Alistair Scott, Dirk-Jan Mattaar, TTphoto; Page 8 © Kils & Marschall 1995; Page 9 © westphalia; Page 10 © TTphoto; Page 12 © Øystein Paulsen; Page 12b © Chris huh; Page 13 © Sam Chadwick, Uwe Kils, Michael Haferkamp; Page 14 © noaa; Page 15 © Joy M. Prescott, Arnold Paul, Uwe kils; Page 16 © Ryerson Clark; Page 17 © Oksana Perkins; Page 18 © Jutta234; Page 19 © Vera Bogaerts; Page 19b © Roger Asbury, Dmitry Deshevykh; Page 20 © Serg Zastavkin; Page 21 © U.S. Fish and Wildlife Service; Page 21b © Roman Krochuk, nialat; Page 22 © Serdar Uckun; Page 23 © Andre Schifer; Page 24 © Tom Kleindinst, Woods Hole Oceanographic Institution, Chris Linder, Woods Hole Oceanographic Institution; Page 25 © Chris Linder, Woods Hole Oceanographic Institution; Page 26 © NOAA; Page 27 © Jan Will; Page 29 © Thomas Pickard
Cover Photos: Glaciers © Vera Bogaerts, Arctic Fox © Sam Chadwick, Arctic Hare © U.S. Fish and Wildlife Service, Arctic Vegetation © Jean-Pierre Lavoie, Arctic Sunlight © AndreyTTL

Editor: Jeanne Sturm

Cover and page design by Nicola Stratford, Blue Door Publishing

Library of Congress Cataloging-in-Publication Data

Hooks, Gwendolyn.
Arctic appetizers : studying food webs in the arctic / Gwendolyn Hooks.
   p. cm. -- (Studying food webs)
 ISBN 978-1-60472-314-4 (hardcover)
 ISBN 978-1-60472-779-1 (softcover)
 1. Ecology--Arctic regions--Juvenile literature. 2. Food chains
(Ecology)--Juvenile literature. I. Title.
 QH84.1.H66 2009

Printed in the USA

CG/CG

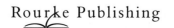

Rourke Publishing

www.rourkepublishing.com – rourke@rourkepublishing.com
Post Office Box 3328, Vero Beach, FL 32964

Table Of Contents

On The Cover

Arctic fox, a predator. Arctic hare is its prey.

Arctic hare, a herbivore, eats vegetation.

Vegetation uses sunlight to make its own food.

Sunlight, the beginning of an arctic food chain.

A Bear of an Ocean

Like a giant bear rambling across the northern sky is the constellation Arktos. Ancient Greeks named the star group Arktos, which means bear. Later, Arktos was changed to Arctic, the name for the ocean surrounding the North Pole and the land surrounding the ocean.

The Arctic Ocean is almost circular and covers an area of about 5,440,000 square miles (14,089,535 square kilometers). It is 13,123 feet (4,000 meters) deep. Unlike other oceans, you can walk on this one. Its ice is about 7 to 10 feet (2 to 3 meters) thick and covers the water most of the year. In some places, the ice never melts.

CHEW ON THIS

The Arctic Ocean surrounds the North Pole. In 1958, the USS Nautilus submarine surfaced through the ice, proving there was not a continent under the North Pole.

Alaska

Canada

ARCTIC OCEAN

Russia

Greenland

Norway   Sweden

Finland

The Arctic Ocean, the Earth's smallest ocean, touches parts of Russia, Finland, Sweden, Norway, Greenland, Canada, and Alaska.

Summer temperatures in this ocean reach about 32 degrees Fahrenheit (0 degrees Celsius). During the winter, the temperature drops to -22 degrees Fahrenheit (-30 degrees Celsius).

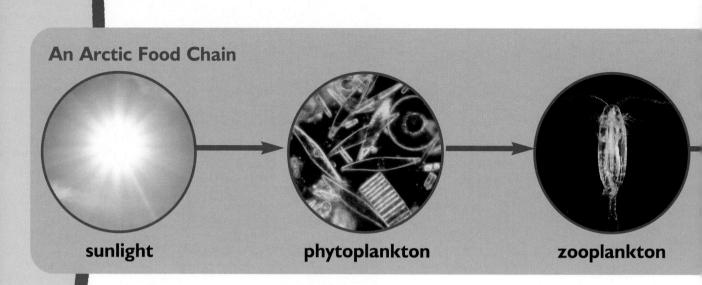

An Arctic Food Chain

sunlight   phytoplankton   zooplankton

Phytoplankton produce food in the Arctic Ocean. They are called **primary producers**. Through **photosynthesis**, a process using sunlight and **nutrients** in the water, phytoplankton produce, or make, food. This is the beginning of a **food chain** of eating and being eaten. Zooplankton are **primary consumers** because they graze on phytoplankton.

Overlapping and interconnected food chains form **food webs**. Food webs show the eating habits of each member of an **ecosystem**. An ecosystem is a combination of all living organisms, such as plants and animals, along with non-living things like the land, water, and the Sun. The Sun provides energy in an ecosystem.

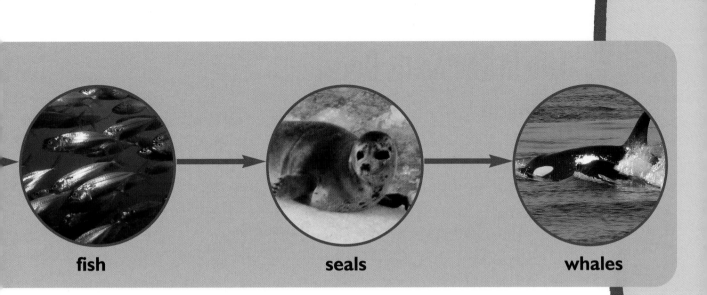

fish   seals   whales

As animals eat, energy is passed from one to the other. The amount of energy decreases as it moves up the chain. Less energy means there are fewer animals at the top levels, since there is not enough food to support more of them.

Arctic terns eat fish. Seals also eat fish. In nature, a food chain has many branches, creating a food web.

Life In The Arctic Ocean

Living in Ice

More than 200 species of ice algae, a type of phytoplankton, thrive in the Arctic. Algae provide food for zooplankton that live in the ice, in open water, and on the sea floor. Zooplankton are herbivores. Herbivores only eat plants.

The arctic ice is pocked with small pores or holes. These holes are less than 0.08 inches (2 millimeters) in diameter and are filled with high levels of salty water called brine.

Ice algae is an important food for zooplankton and other organisms. Ice algae will eventually break off and fall to the ocean floor, where it will be eaten by animals living on or under the ocean floor.

Icebreakers have the power to move through icy arctic waters.

CHEW ON THIS

Permanent ice in the Arctic Ocean is called polar ice. The ice that freezes around the edges of polar ice during the winter months is pack ice.

The arctic ice serves as a nursery for young zooplankton. It provides a barrier between the extreme cold on the surface and the sea water below. As summer approaches, the ice begins to melt. The zooplankton are released into the water, providing food for other zooplankton and fish.

Long ago, early explorers believed the Arctic Ocean couldn't support life. Modern scientists have proven them wrong.

CHEW ON THIS

Zooplankton are primary consumers, the first animals in ocean food chains. Since arctic cod eat zooplankton, they are secondary consumers.

Seals chill out on the ice between hunting trips.

The ocean floor is made of underwater mountain ridges and deep trenches. Benthos refers to life on the ocean floor. Unlike plants and algae that must live in shallow water for sunlight to reach them, animals can live on the ocean floor. Scientists believe their survival on the ocean floor depends more on the food that drifts down to them than the cold temperatures.

The arctic continental shelves receive more food than the deepest part of the ocean. This would explain why bottom feeders like the gray whales frequent continental shelves.

The global continental shelf. The arctic continental shelf is above the red dotted line.

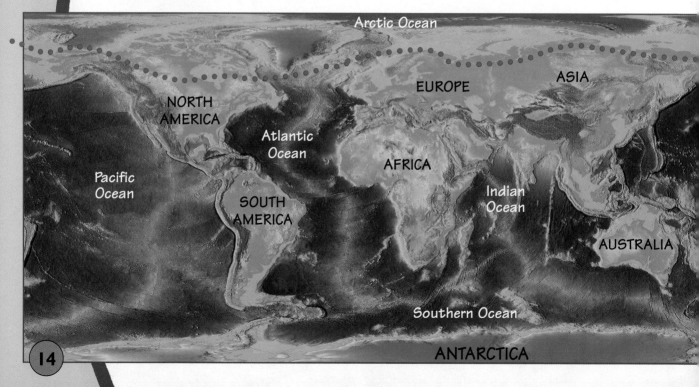

sand flea

bristle worm

Sand fleas, bristle worms, and bivalve mollusks are examples of animals that live on the continental shelves. Some of them live inside the sediment. They are called infauna, which means animals living in the sediment.

Mussels are a type of bivalve mollusk.

Arctic Tundra

The arctic tundra is frozen nearly year round. Most of the soil is permanently frozen and is called **permafrost**. Permafrost is about 9 to 35 inches (23 to 89 cm) deep.

During the winter it's dark and cold. The temperature is about -18 degrees Fahrenheit (-28 degrees Celsius). In the summer, the temperature is about 54 degrees Fahrenheit (12 degrees Celsius). It is extremely windy with little precipitation.

The arctic tundra is treeless with only short shrubs and other low growing plants. Because the arctic tundra gets so little precipitation, it's often called a cold desert.

During the tundra summer, the soggy ground forms marshes, lakes, and bogs that attract migrating birds.

CHEW ON THIS

Mosquitoes don't freeze on the tundra because they replace the water in their body with glycerol. Glycerol allows them to survive the winter under the snow. During the summer, mosquitoes can make the tundra a miserable place.

Tundra Plants

Arctic plants are small and grow close to the ground. Mosses, lichens, shrubs, and heaths are examples of plants that have adapted to the tundra conditions.

During the summer, the top layer of the soil thaws out so that plants can grow and reproduce.

Permafrost prevents tree roots from growing deep into the soil. The willow will only grow about 3 inches (7.6 centimeters) tall and looks more like ground cover than a tree.

Arctic lichens and bearberry leaves.

Tundra plants depend on animal droppings to add nutrients to the soil.

Wolverines have jaws strong
enough to bite through frozen
meat and bone.

Wolves and wolverines are the top **predators** on the tundra. They are meat eating animals. Meat eaters are called **carnivores**. They feed on smaller animals like snowshoe hares and lemmings.

Arctic squirrels are **omnivores**. Omnivores eat both plants and animals. Their usual diet consists of seeds, roots, and fruit. If they are starving, they will eat insects and **carrion**.

Arctic ground squirrels live in colonies and are the only arctic animal that hibernates.

The snowshoe hare has large rear feet with toes that spread out like snowshoes. For camouflage, its fur turns white during the winter and rusty brown during the summer.

Large herds of caribou live on the tundra. They are herbivores that feed on plants. They eat tender willow leaves, flowering plants, and mushrooms in the summer. During winter months, caribou eat lichens and small shrubs.

Breaking It Down

Arctic bacteria are **decomposers**. They break down dead plants and animals into nutrients. This occurs in the water column and on the ocean floor. Algae utilize the nutrients during photosynthesis.

Bacteria are not the only source for nutrients. Some nutrients have been transported from rivers that empty into the ocean. Other nutrients are pushed up from the ocean floor. Some nutrients are deposited from the atmosphere.

Scientists collect ice and water samples to study the algae and bacteria.

CHEW ON THIS

When the Sun exits the Arctic during the winter, and algae is scarce, bacteria steps in as the primary producer.

Working On Ice

Spending summers on Buzzards Bay in Massachusetts sparked Dr. Carin Ashjian's interest in the ocean. She kept her interest alive by studying biological oceanography. That's the study of ocean plants and animals and how they are affected by their environment.

Dr. Carin Ashjian

Now Dr. Ashjian spends her summers studying zooplankton aboard research ships in the Arctic Ocean. One study involved four different species of copepods, a type of zooplankton. Dr. Ashjian wanted to learn more about their role in the Arctic food web, how they reproduce, and how many of each species live in the water column. She believes that understanding a species will help predict how it will survive climate changes.

Carin Ashjian and Daniel Gaona deploy a ring net off the fantail of the Healy.

A science party from the Canadian Coast Guard icebreaker Louis S. St. Laurent installs instruments on arctic sea ice that monitor ocean, ice, and atmospheric conditions and transmit data daily via satellite.

SHRINKING ICE!

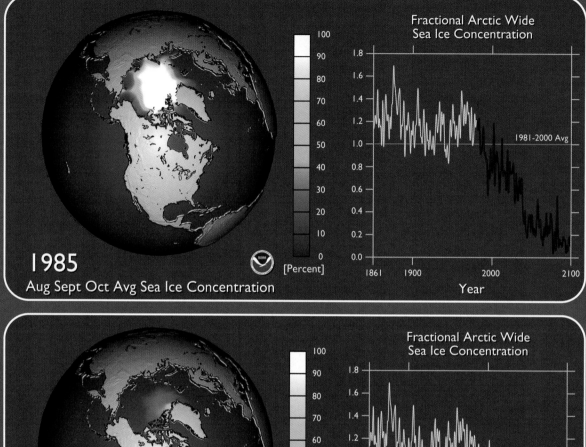

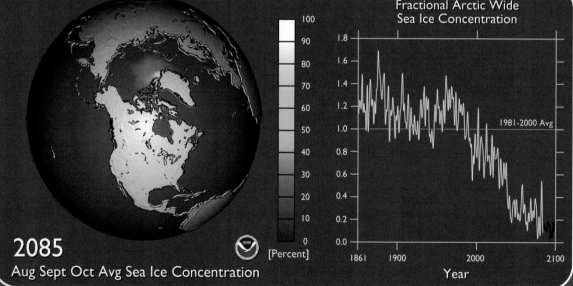

The top picture shows ice thickness in the Arctic in 1985. The bottom picture shows NOAA's prediction of the ice thickness in 2085. (NOAA stands for *The National Oceanic and Atmospheric Administration*)

What happens in the Arctic has far-reaching effects. Melting arctic ice causes sea levels to rise. Over the last 20 years, sea levels have risen about 3 inches (7 to 8 centimeters). Some scientists predict sea levels will rise from 4 inches (10 centimeters) to 3 feet (91 centimeters) during the next 100 years.

Disappearing sea ice leads to starving polar bears since they hunt seals from the ice. Scientists are finding more drowned polar bears than ever before.

Greenhouse gases refer to gases in the Earth's atmosphere. Water vapor, carbon dioxide, and methane are examples of greenhouse gases. They act like the glass of a greenhouse and help to warm the Earth. People are burning more and more **fossil fuels**. This causes greenhouse gases to increase, leading to global warming.

CHEW ON THIS

Since ringed seals use the ice to give birth and raise their young, less ice means lower survival rates.

The Arctic Ocean and the arctic tundra are showing the effects of people's actions. Mining, drilling, and pollution are changing what was once a clean and clear environment.

How You Can Help:
- For short distances, walk, or use a bike instead of a car.
- Turn off lights, televisions, computers, and other electrical appliances when you are not using them.
- Play outside games.
- Plant trees.
- Recycle household items like plastic milk bottles and soda cans.
- Lower air conditioning use by closing curtains to block the sun.
- Lower heating use by wearing warmer clothing in layers.
- Wait for large loads before using the washing machine and dishwasher.

Together, with everyone helping, the Arctic can continue to support life, from the largest whales to the smallest bit of algae.

Glossary

carnivores (KAR-nuh-vorz): animals that eat other animals

carrion (KAIR-ee-yon): bodies of dead animals

decomposers (dee-cum-POH-zerz): animals and plants that cause rot and decay, enriching the soil with valuable nutrients

ecosystem (EE-koh-sis-tum): the relationships between all the plants and animals and the place in which they live

food chain (FOOD CHAYN): a series of plants and animals, each of which is eaten by the one after it

food web (FOOD WEHB): in an ecosystem, the intricate network of food chains

fossil fuels (FAH-suhl FYU-uhlz): fuels such as natural gas, oil, and coal that were formed millions of years ago from plant and animal remains

native (NAY-tiv): naturally occurring, living in the place where it originated

nutrients (NOO-tree-uhnts): the substances that plants and animals need to grow

omnivores (AHM-nih-vorz): animals that feed on a wide variety of foods including both plants and animals

permafrost (PUR-muh-frawst): the land that is permanently frozen in the tundra

photosynthesis (foh-toh-SIN-thuh-siss): the process by which green plants transform the Sun's energy into food

predators (PRED-uh-turz): animals that hunt other animals for food

primary consumers (PRYE-mair-ee kahn-SOO-merz): herbivores, the animals that feed on primary producers

primary producers (PRYE-mair-ee proh-DOO-serz): plants that perform photosynthesis

Further Reading

Want to learn more about Arctic food webs? The following books and websites are a great place to start!

Books

Lynch, Wayne. *The Arctic.* NorthWord Books for Young Readers, 2007.

Vekteris, Donna. *Scholastic Atlas of Oceans.* New York, 2004.

Vogel, Carole Garbuny. *Ocean Wildlife, The Restless Sea.*
  Franklin Watts, 2003.

Websites

Icebreakers
http://www.natice.noaa.gov/icebreakers/index.htm

Arctic and Antarctica Activity Book
http://coastalscience.noaa.gov/education/aabook.pdf

Polar Bears-Smithsonian Institution
http://www.mnh.si.edu/arctic/game/index.html

Secrets of the Ocean Realm
http://www.pbs.org/oceanrealm/

Index

About the Author

Gwendolyn Hooks has been an avid reader all of her life. When she was a child and supposed to be asleep, Gwendolyn sat by her window and used the streetlight to read "just one more chapter." Gwendolyn graduated from the University of Missouri-St. Louis with an education degree. Still an avid reader, she now writes fiction and nonfiction for children. This is her seventh book for young readers. She has three adult children and lives in Oklahoma City with her husband.